Traversing Time

The Science of Time Travel and Chronodynamics

Table of Contents

Chapter 1. Introduction

In our Special Report titled "Traversing Time: The Science of Time Travel and Chronodynamics," we delve into a subject that has intrigued scientists, philosophers, and avid science-fiction enthusiasts alike. While time travel often occupies a space more commonly associated with the realms of cinematic storytelling and speculative fiction, our report is designed to ground these concepts in the profound and intriguing science behind them. We untangle the complex theories and hard-core physics, and distill them into an easy-to-grasp exploration of the potential reality of moving through time. Drawing on the theories of famous scientists along with cutting-edge research, we invite you to journey with us - not just into the realms of possibility, but into a fascinating universe where science weaves together the fabric of time. If intrigued by the mysteries of the cosmos and the endless possibilities of time travel, this report is your gateway to unlock a world limited only by the boundaries of time itself. Get ready to step into the fourth dimension from the comfort of your living room! The future (and past) awaits...

Chapter 2. Unravelling Time: An Introduction

In the beginning, there was time. Even before the birth of the universe some 13.8 billion years ago in the Big Bang, time had its existence, albeit in a state and dimension that our human minds find hard to perceive. As we journey onward, recognize that, unlike space, time transcends the standard three physical dimensions we live in. It constitutes the oft-spoken about fourth dimension in the phenomenon we call 'spacetime'. This invisible flow of time governs the universe and our lives - progressing unyieldingly forward and offering no option to revisit the past or pre-visit the future.

2.1. The Concept of Time

Humans have always been fascinated with the concept of time. Ancient civilizations strove to understand it, marking the apparent cycles of the sun, moon, and seasons. Early timekeeping devices like the sundials and hourglasses have evolved into the incredibly precise atomic and quantum clocks of today. Yet, the fundamental nature of time remains an enigma.

Relatively recently, within the past couple of centuries, our understanding of time has transformed radically thanks to two revolutionary theories submitted by perhaps the greatest scientific mind of the 20th century, Albert Einstein: Special and General Relativity.

2.2. Time and Relativity

To unravel the mysteries of time, it is crucial to understand these theories. Starting with Special Relativity, Einstein stated that the laws of physics are the same for all observers, regardless of their relative motion. This results in surprising effects. For example, a stationary observer will perceive time to move slower for a moving observer; this is called 'time dilation'.

General Relativity further incorporates gravity into this picture, suggesting that matter and energy "curve" spacetime, causing objects to move on this curved path and slower time near massive bodies - 'gravitational time dilation'.

2.2.1. Time Dilation

The effect of time dilation, both due to speed and gravity, has been confirmed through several experiments. Take for example the case of GPS satellites. They are far above the Earth and travel at high speeds, meaning, according to General Relativity, their clocks should run faster. But they are also in a weaker gravitational field than we are on Earth, so their clocks should run slower. The net effect is that they run faster, and engineers must adjust for this difference to ensure GPS works as intended.

2.3. Is Time Travel Possible?

Taking the implications of these theories further, one might imagine that if time could be dilated, could it also be traversed? Could we travel into the past or future? This idea hinges on solutions to Einstein's General Relativity equations, known as 'wormholes' and 'cosmic strings.'

2.3.1. Wormholes

Wormholes are theoretically allowed in General Relativity. They can be envisioned as a bridge or tunnel through spacetime, connecting two distant points almost instantaneously. If a wormhole could be kept stable, which current physics suggests would require 'exotic' matter with negative energy density, traveling through it could effectively be a form of time travel. However, wormholes are still entirely theoretical and yet to be observed.

2.3.2. Cosmic Strings

Cosmic strings are enormously massive, thinner than an atomic nucleus, and hypothetically left over from the early universe. If two such strings passed close to each other, they could bend space-time strongly enough to create a loop for time travel. But again, even their existence, let alone manipulating them for time travel, remains theoretical.

2.4. Looking into the Future

Only time (and much more scientific discovery) will tell if the grand concept of time travel can be made a reality. Though we haven't mastered the ability to traverse time in the manner of science fiction heroes just yet, our growing understanding of the universe presents limitless possibilities.

This journey into chronodynamics may raise as many questions as it answers. Is time a fundamental constant of the cosmos, or is it merely a human construct? Could we ever master time to the point where past, present, and future are open to us at will?

Our time together is just getting started. Whether we ever decipher the true nature of time or we simply deepen the puzzle, the quest to understand and harness time remains one of the grandest dreams of science. And each seeking spirit, every astute mind that delves into this realm with curiosity and rigorous science, takes us one step closer to new findings, insights, and realities yet to be unravelled. The journey continues in our next chapter...

Chapter 3. The Principals behind Chronodynamics

In the journey to fully understanding the principles of chronodynamics, it's critical to lay the cornerstone well - by providing a solid rudimentary understanding of time itself. Narratives from popular scientific literature usually start with the concept of space-time, conceptualized so eloquently by Albert Einstein in his theory of General Relativity. It's a four-dimensional continuum, with three dimensions of space and one dimension of time.

3.1. Space-time and Time dilation

Einstein suggested that space-time has a great impact on our perception and measurement of time. He posited that space isn't separate from time, but intricately entwined with it. This radical and novel concept proposed that time can slow down or speed up depending on the intensity of the gravitational field, a phenomenon called 'time dilation'. This effect has been verified numerous times in experiments involving highly accurate atomic clocks. For instance, a clock closer to a massive object (and thus with a stronger gravitational field) ticks slower compared to an identical one positioned further away.

3.2. The Twin Paradox

The practical example of time dilation forms the basis of the so-called 'Twin Paradox'. Imagine twins, one of whom embarks on a round-trip voyage to a distant star, traveling close to the speed of light. When the traveling twin returns, she might find her earth-bound sibling has aged more than she has. This isn't just a theoretical thought experiment - it's a reality that has been empirically verified in several experiments, the most notable being the Hafele-Keating experiment using atomic clocks and commercial airlines in 1971.

3.3. The Mathematics of Time Travel

Now let's delve into the equations that govern these phenomena. Einstein's field equations quite literally govern the "lay of the land" in spacetime, dictating how matter and energy shape it. These equations fundamentally assert that gravity emanates from matter and energy present in spacetime, causing it to curve. This curvature then influences the movement of matter and energy in spacetime. It's this very curvature that becomes important when we consider the possibility of routes or 'wormholes' that could enable time travel.

3.4. Wormholes and Chronology Protection Conjecture

Wormholes are shortcuts through spacetime, connecting otherwise distant points. Theoretically, if one could harness the power to keep a wormhole stable against collapse, one could facilitate time travel - a concept you might recognize from many a science-fiction plot. Currently, though, there's no practical or experimental proof of the existence of such wormholes.

The concept of time travel often confronts another principle formulated by Stephen Hawking - the 'Chronology Protection Conjecture'. This hypothesis states that the laws of physics will conspire to prevent time travel on a macroscopic scale, shielding the universe from the dangers of causality violations, such as the infamous paradox where one travels back in time and kills one's own grandparent!

3.5. Quantum Mechanics and Time

Quantum mechanics, another pillar of modern physics, brings a slightly different perspective to the table. The Feynman path integral formulation, for instance, allows processes that can be traced backward as well as forward in time. Many interpretations of quantum mechanics, like the Many-Worlds Interpretation, theoretically provide frameworks that allow for 'quantum time travel' without causality paradoxes.

However, it's critical to understand that while tremendously promising, these interpretations and formulations are fledgling and much research is needed to validate or negate these theories.

3.6. The Road Ahead

The current landscape of chronodynamics is vast and continually evolving, painting a tantalizing picture of potential time travel. The mathematical underpinnings of the concept, although still in a stage of flux, add credibility to this captivating possibility.

However, until we can resolve the conflicting aspects of quantum mechanics and general relativity, many questions about time and time travel will remain unanswered. Expeditions into the realm of string theory and quantum gravity promise exciting advances, potentially unifying the two discordant theories, and bringing us closer to understanding – and perhaps even mastering – time itself.

It's safe to say that the journey is only just commencing. With diligent systematic exploration, the possibilities within the discipline of chronodynamics may one day stretch the fabric of our understanding in ways we haven't even begun to conceive. Laymen and scientists alike can only watch with bated breath as the grand chronodrama of chronodynamics unfolds.

Chapter 4. Time and Space: An Intertwined Relationship

Beginnings can be found in small places, places as unassuming and yet as colossal as the Planck length, named for the physicist Max Planck who first suggested this scale – a scale so infinitesimally tiny, it's considered the 'grain' of our universe. To put this into perspective, if a particle or dot about 0.1 millimetres in size (the smallest thing the naked eye can manage to perceive) were magnified to the size of the observable universe, then inside that universe-sized 'dot,' the Planck length would equate to an actual 0.1 millimetre dot. It is where our classical (Galilean) understandings of space and time must bend to the often less intuitive theories of quantum physics, opening a can-of-worms we have just begun to understand.

4.1. The Dance of Time and Space: A Ballet of Cosmic Proportions

Einstein's Theory of Relativity led to the realization that space and time are not separate entities, but instead mingled in one four-dimensional continuum, rightfully known as spacetime. Here, space constitutes the previously understood three dimensions, while time provides the tricky fourth. In this domain, time doesn't tick away uniformly as we've come to think, but instead, it's influenced by mass and velocity. Large masses, like planets, distort spacetime—akin to a bowling ball on a trampoline. Any object passing nearby, say a marble, would roll and spiral downwards, reflecting the warping of spacetime.

Likewise, time ticks slower the closer you are to a massive body, a phenomenon evidenced by the aging of two identical atomic clocks displaying different times: one at high altitude and another at sea level – an experiment brilliantly demonstrating Einstein's gravitational time dilation.

4.2. Warped Space - Warped Time

Stephen Hawking brought spacetime to the general consciousness, painting a picture of a universe bubbling with 'wormholes' – shortcuts through spacetime. These hypothetical tunnels propose a mind-bending means for traveling great distances across space and time. While they're rooted in relativity, the reality of their existence remains a mystery. Melding general relativity with quantum mechanics could potentially crack the conundrum.

However, these wormholes aren't our conventional 'tunnels.' Traveling through them might require contending with violations of causality (i.e., causing an effect before its cause), entering other universes, or other bizarre effects that boggle even the surest scientific minds.

4.3. The Quantum Realm – Until Planck Scale Do Us Part

The discord between Einstein's relativity (a beautiful theory explaining the macro universe) and quantum theory (explaining the behaviours at Planck scales) is striking when we descend into the relativistic quantum world – the world on a subatomic scale wherein time and space become far more mysterious than we could have ever imagined.

Quantum theory suggests that there is no 'time' at these miniature scales, at least not as we understand it. Instead, interactions are affected by weird and less intuitive concepts, like 'superposition' where particles exist in multiple states simultaneously, only adopting a definitive state when observed.

Furthermore, dominant forces at these scales, like quantum

entanglement – a peculiar phenomenon where entangled particles exhibit matching properties regardless of their separation, seemingly communicating faster than the speed of light – is something even Einstein described as "spooky action at a distance".

4.4. Traversing Through Time: The Realities and Impediments

Time Travel has often been theoretically posited using wormholes. However, a voyage through a wormhole isn't as simple as stepping through a door. According to physicist Kip Thorne, while it's theoretically possible to travel through a wormhole, sustaining them would require 'exotic' matter with negative energy density. Even then, the journey might be perilous or one-way.

Relativity provides loopholes, like the 'twins paradox,' hinting that time travel might be possible under specific conditions. The twins paradox involves a scenario where one twin travels near light speed on a spaceship, then returns to find the other twin aged more, thus positing that moving near light speed can take us to the future.

Yet, going back remains a conundrum. Also, practical difficulties - such as acquiring the energy to approach light speed or constructing a wormhole - along with paradoxes it might introduce, render actual time travel currently impossible.

4.5. Chaos, Order, and Time's Arrow

Finally, the 'arrow of time' - the direction of time from past to future - brings another layer of intricacy. While laws of physics don't discriminate between forward and reverse, our experience of time flow decidedly does. This conflict can be attributed to thermodynamics. According to the second law of thermodynamics, the universe tends towards 'entropy' - or disorder. An egg will break and scramble but won't unscramble and reassemble, drawing a clear line between past and future.

Physicist Sean Carroll's theory suggests that the Big Bang started the universe in a low-entropy state, and ever since, it's been increasing, thereby manufacturing the 'arrow of time.'

4.6. The Clock Ticks On

The scientific journey towards understanding the nature of time and space continues beyond these realms, with current initiatives in 'loop quantum gravity' and 'string theory' promising to bring us closer to the elusive 'theory of everything.' No matter how arduous the journey, it is the sheer joy of discovery that pushes us onward.

Chapter 5. Concluding Remarks

The gargantuan dance of time and space is an ever-unfolding ballet, one we're just beginning to understand, let alone control or navigate. As we discern more, questions will inevitably arise, questions that punctuate our eagerness to understand, experiment, and most importantly, to know what time truly is. For now, time travel remains a fascinating theoretical realm, relegated to the speculative world of science fiction.

However, in the future, who can say for certain that the line between reality and science fiction will remain so rigidly definite? Perhaps we are on the precipice of an immense revolution in our understanding of time and space, where the impossible becomes possible, and the universe as we know it becomes a treasure trove of uncharted potentialities. Only 'time' will reveal...

Chapter 6. Einstein's Relativity: The Foundation of Time Travel

The path to understanding time travel goes through the intricate terrain of Albert Einstein's theory of relativity. Developed in the early 20th century, this critical doctrine reshaped our perceptions of time and space, introducing concepts integral for grasping the probabilities of time travel.

Einstein's relativity is divided into two parts: the special theory of relativity and the general theory of relativity. While the former deals with space-time in environments devoid of gravity, the latter accounts for the curved nature of space-time due to the mass and energy within. Both theories are fundamental to understanding the crux of time travel.

6.1. The Special Theory of Relativity

The special theory of relativity is rooted primarily in two postulates. The first posits that the laws of physics remain the same in all inertial frames of reference. The second argues that the speed of light 'c' in a vacuum is constant and is the same in all frames of reference, irrespective of the relative motion of the observer or the light source.

Einstein built from these axioms to develop profound inferences regarding time, including the phenomena of time dilation and length contraction. These are concepts that sound as though they belong in science fiction, but they are already confirmed aspects of our physical reality. Schrodinger's train thought experiment helps us visualize this.

Consider two observers, A and B, with A situated on the ground and

B in a fast-moving train. B decides to perform a simple light experiment. He sets up a light beam apparatus that reflects a light beam from the bottom to the top of the train carriage, then back to the bottom. B argues that according to him, the light in his experiment moved in a straight line up and then down - creating no deviation.

However, observer A, watching from the platform, sees matters differently. From A's point of view, the train carriage moved while the light traveled up and down. As such, A visualizes the light beam taking a diagonal forward path while ascending and a diagonal backward path while descending.

Consequently, A and B disagree about the distance the light beam traveled. For B, the distance is simply twice the height of the carriage. For A, using Pythagoras's theorem, it's the square root of the sum of the squares of the carriage's height and the distance the train moved while the light beam was in transit.

The speed of light is constant, so the travel time for light must adapt to preserve the second postulate. As such, time appears to have dilated for B in his moving reference frame. This fascinating phenomenon is known as time dilation and is a fundamental element that supports the principle of time travel.

6.2. The General Theory of Relativity

Next, we delve into the general theory of relativity (GR). Simply put, it extends the principle of special relativity to scenarios involving gravity. Einstein introduced this landmark theory in 1915, ten years after his special relativity. It presents an entirely new paradigm to understand gravity, positioning it not as a force akin to others but a fundamental feature of the universe's geometry.

According to GR, the existence of matter and energy causes spacetime to curve. Objects moving in spacetime follow this curvature, which, from an external viewpoint, seems to be the action of a gravitational 'force'. The more the mass and energy, the more pronounced is the curvature, and hence, the stronger is the gravitational effect.

There's a drastic implication relating to time. Time, similar to space, is also subject to the curvature of spacetime. This 'warped' time leads to the phenomenon called gravitational time dilation. Time is observed to move slower in a high gravitational field (near a massive object) as compared to a lower gravitational field.

This has been observed experimentally with atomic clocks placed at different altitudes. Clocks at a higher altitude (lower gravity) run faster than clocks placed at a lower altitude (higher gravity). While the difference is minuscule, it's significant, especially in systems like GPS, where high precision timings are necessary.

6.3. Time Travel and Relativity

With discussions of time dilation and the malleability of spacetime, one might consider the leap to time travel a straightforward one. Not really; time indeed appears to be more flexible under relativity, but the extent of this flexibility remains a subject of much debate and current research.

One concept proposed as a gateway to potential time travel is the idea of wormholes. These are essentially 'tunnels' through spacetime - shortcuts that connect different points in spacetime. If found or created, wormholes would potentially provide a dramatic realization of time travel.

However, the existence and stability of wormholes is as yet unproven and is a contentious topic among theoreticians. Following relativity, creating or maintaining a wormhole may require 'exotic' forms of matter or energy with negative energy density - a state that is extremely challenging (if not impossible) in our current understanding of physics.

Einstein's theory of relativity has thus lent us a framework to approach the concept of time travel. Though it does not provide a definitive means to achieve it, its potential suggestions have greatly inspired the imaginations of physicists and science fiction writers alike. The prospect of travel through time, as implied by these theories, offers exciting avenues to explore in our understanding of the universe.

Through Einstein's theories, we have come to perceive time in a more fluid, less absolute way, much different from our everyday experiences. This gives us the impetus to delve deeper into our investigation into the titillating possibility of time travel. And who knows? The day might come when the boundaries between fact and fiction blur, and we might figure out a way to traverse the corridors of time.

Chapter 7. Wormholes: Pathways through Time?

Time travel has intoxicated humanity's imagination for generations, compelling a vast array of depictions from H.G. Wells' 'The Time Machine' to the 'Doctor Who' series. However, what if these fictions aren't solely the realm of imaginings, but instead, grounded on scientific principles? The concept doesn't sound so far-fetched when you consider wormholes, mysterious entities that provide pathways through time and space. This section focuses on this topic, shedding light on the fundamentals and latest discoveries.

7.1. The Theory of Wormholes

Let's start with the basics: a wormhole, in theoretical physics, is a feature of spacetime that could be a shortcut between distinct points in time and space. Attributed initially to Albert Einstein and Nathan Rosen, wormholes were extrapolated in 1935 from the general theory of relativity as bridges connecting two separate patches of spacetime, later termed 'Einstein-Rosen bridges'.

Contrary to popular depictions, wormholes aren't tunnels in the conventional sense. Instead, they are deformations of the spacetime fabric. Consider spacetime as a two-dimensional sheet, a supposed flat 'universe'. A wormhole can be visualized as someone bending that sheet over, enabling relocation from one point to another through a hypothetical bridge, thus bypassing the otherwise typically traversed 'space'.

7.2. Stability of Wormholes

While wormholes may sound like a fantastic means for interstellar travel, they are far from stable passages. Predictions from Einstein's general theory of relativity indicate that they would instantly collapse upon formation, hardly surviving long enough for anything to pass through. This issue signifies the unstable nature of wormholes, and their existence solely relies on speculative forms of matter with negative energy density, often termed 'exotic matter'.

Nevertheless, questions remain. First, exotic matter is purely theoretical and has yet to be detected. Second, even if it does exist, acquiring the necessary amounts to stabilize a wormhole would likely surpass the total energy of all the matter in the known universe. Finally, if a technique of acquiring such exotic matter was indeed found, keeping the wormhole open would require an energy equivalent at least to a star.

7.3. Wormholes and Quantum Physics

A shift in perspective from the macro to the micro might render wormholes slightly more accessible. Quantum physics, specifically quantum mechanics and quantum field theory, put forth a scenario where wormhole-like 'quantum tunnels' may be plausible.

Quantum mechanics posits strange rules, allowing subatomic particles to 'tunnel' through barriers despite inadequate kinetic energy. Analogously, one could imagine 'quantum tunnels' in spacetime itself. Quantum foam, an idea supported by quantum field theory, contends that the smallest scales of spacetime are bubbling with minute wormholes and temporary particle-antiparticle pairs, thus potentially enabling very small-scale time travel.

However, should we wish to scale these quantum wormholes up to human size, the previous problems arising from general relativity persist – how to stabilize these ephemeral wormholes?

7.4. Wormholes: Fantasy or Reality?

Despite the limitations, optimism for wormholes as possible time travel conduits persists. Some scientists posit that wormholes might already exist at the cosmological scale, fashioned by the universe's expansion over billions of years. Some also propose that advanced civilizations could generate wormholes and stabilize them by mastering negative energy manipulation.

But until such hypothesizing finds grounding in empirical evidence, wormholes remain firmly lodged in the realms of theory and fiction. Yet who knows? As our understanding of the universe evolves, we may one day unravel spacetime's secrets and perhaps find the ultimate key, opening the temporal gates through wormholes.

In summary, our journey through the wormhole concept exposes the intriguing, slightly arcane science of time travel. For now, wormholes remain intangible, a concept nestled between the brilliance of mathematical equations and the boundless realm of imaginative speculation. However, the allure of leaping through time and space ensures that wormholes will continue to captivate researchers, driving them to unlock the mysteries. After all, piecing together the universe's puzzles forms the heart of our human venture, a thirst to understand, explore, and perhaps, to traverse time.

Chapter 8. Tachyons and Quantum Physics: The Edge of Understanding

Let's start with the basic premise on which our understanding of the universe and its fundamental mechanics rests. Physics, as we know, is divided into two broad categories: General Relativity, dealing with the macroscopic universe, and Quantum Mechanics, dealing with the minuscule atomic and subatomic particles. Confronting these two theories can lead to what we refer to as quantum gravity, a realm where one day we may be able to explain the large-scale structure of the cosmos and the tiny buzzing world of particles and fields in one grand theory. And right there, at the edge of this understanding, we encounter Tachyons.

8.1. Understanding Tachyons

Tachyons are traditionally described as hypothetical particles that travel faster than the speed of light. Such particles appear to violate the cosmic speed limit set by Einstein's theory of relativity, which posits that nothing can surpass the speed of light. Yet, not all versions of tachyons transgress the established laws of Physics. Some interactions within Quantum Field Theory (QFT), a pillar of modern physics, seem to allow for the existence of these peculiar particles, albeit in a slightly modified and mitigated version.

Tachyons, if they exist, could be a solution to quantum field theory equations that possess "imaginary" mass. In contrast to the familiar "real" mass, imaginary mass isn't a concept we deal with in everyday physics. It is a mathematical feature that arises from the square root operation when dealing with negative numbers—a somewhat cumbersome quirk of the mathematics rather than a quirk of nature.

A common misconception is that tachyons could be employed to send information backward in time, but it's essential to note that this isn't quite accurate. Because the interactions of tachyons are not well defined, the transmission of information using them would likely be random and chaotic, not useful for communication.

8.2. The Role of Quantum Physics

Quantum mechanics forms one of the key theoretical frameworks that makes the concept of tachyons viable, albeit in limited circumstances. The fundamental crux of quantum theory is that of uncertainty, with the Heisenberg uncertainty principle at its heart. Simply put, this principle states that it's impossible to simultaneously measure the precise position and momentum (or energy and time) of a particle.

Now, through the probabilistic interpretation of the quantum wave function, we know that a particle can exist in multiple states or places at once. This superposition principle underlies our understanding of the strange quantum world, giving us a glimmer of the possibilities that could make certain kinds of time travel feasible.

The supposed existence of tachyons, combined with the uncertainty and superposition principles of quantum mechanics, might produce intriguing situations where certain quantum processes could result in outcomes that apparently precede their causes. However, this "quantum weirdness" does not violate causality in any practical sense. Instead, it underscores the significant discrepancies between quantum mechanics and general relativity, highlighting the ongoing challenges in unifying the two theories.

8.3. Implications of Tachyons in Quantum Field Theory

Even if we do not consider tachyons as physical particles, their hypothetical existence has profound implications for quantum field theory.

Firstly, the occurrence of tachyonic solutions in a given field implies an instability in that field. The field desires to lower its energy, often resulting in a phenomenon known as symmetry breaking, a feature inherent to many important theories, including the Higgs Mechanism.

Secondly, tachyonic fields play a crucial role in the early universe's cosmology, notably in theories of cosmic inflation. The concept of inflation posits that the universe underwent a rapid exponential expansion shortly after the Big Bang, driven by the energy of a scalar field (a field that is the same everywhere and in all directions). Some cosmologists propose that this field could have tachyonic properties.

From tachyonic fields' employment in describing real-world phenomena like spontaneous symmetry breaking, to their potential theorized role in cosmic inflation, the implications of tachyons are far-reaching, despite their hypothetical nature.

8.4. Tachyons and Time Travel

The lore of tachyons often involves their association with time travel potentially. After all, a particle which inherently travels faster than light might naturally pique interest in the temporal domain. However, it's important to separate the exoticism of tachyons from reality.

While tachyons in their raw form would indeed provide a fascinating prospect for time travel or faster-than-light communication, the true nature of tachyons—if they exist at all—indicates a far more complex reality. Yet, this doesn't rule out the captivating possibility of time travel.

Looking at the principles of quantum mechanics in conjunction with the presence of time-like curves in the solutions of Einstein's equations, we arrive at a promising landscape for the possibilities of time travel. Yet, mapping such theoretical entities into our macroscopic world presents a whole other challenge.

Will we ever harness the magic of quantum physics and tachyons to traverse through time? The answer remains elusive as the science continues to evolve.

By delving into the edges of our understanding with tachyons and quantum physics, we are not only expanding our grasp of the universe but also paving the way for staggering possibilities in the realm of understanding time as we know it. Thus, the exploration of these intricate layers of reality not only pushes the boundaries of our knowledge but also elevates our grasp towards the elusive fourth dimension.

Chapter 9. Challenges and Paradoxes in Time Travel

Before we start probing into the challenges time travel presents, let's dive into the physics that provides its very foundation. The concept of time travel is deeply rooted in Albert Einstein's theory of relativity, more specifically, in the theories of special and general relativity.

To put it in simple terms, special relativity tells us that time slows down for an object moving at speeds approaching the speed of light. If a person travels at rates near light speed, time will slow down for them in relation to those who have remained stationary (according to their own perception). This is typically referred to as "time dilation," a scientifically accepted truth that has been verified by numerous experiments.

General relativity, on the other hand, describes the relationship between mass and space. It explains gravity as the warping or distorting of spacetime around massive objects. In terms of time travel, general relativity presents the idea of "wormholes," which are theoretical bridges through spacetime that could potentially provide a shortcut to a distant location or time.

While these concepts are fascinating, numerous challenges and paradoxes arise as we search for realistic mechanisms of time travel. Let's navigate through them in the sections below.

9.1. The Grandfather Paradox

One of the most popular thought experiments concerning time travel is the Grandfather Paradox. This thought experiment raises a question about going back in time and changing past events. If you travel back to a time when your grandfather was young and prevent him from meeting your grandmother, it gives rise to an apparent inconsistency. If he never met your grandmother, then one of your parents would not be born, neither would you. If you were never born, how could you have traveled back in time in the first place?

9.2. The Bootstrap Paradox

Next on our journey of paradoxes is the Bootstrap Paradox or a causal loop. It's a scenario where an object or piece of information sent back in time results in an infinite loop where the item doesn't have a discernible point of origin. For instance, a man receives a book from a time traveler that was published in the future. He reads it and later republishes it word for word. Another traveler takes this book back to the original man. So, who wrote the book originally?

9.3. The Twin Paradox

Exploring further, we stumble upon the Twin Paradox, a thought experiment resulting from the theory of special relativity. One twin boards a spaceship and journeys into space at speeds close to light, while the other remains on Earth. Upon returning, the traveling twin is significantly younger than the Earth-bound twin. This paradox challenges our intuitive understanding of time but is theoretically possible according to special relativity.

9.4. Time Travelling at the Speed of Light

Outside the realm of paradoxes, we face the massive challenge of achieving the speeds required for time dilation to have a significant effect. The speed of light, fundamental to theories of time travel, is an enormous 299,792 kilometers per second. No spaceship built to date can achieve even a fraction of this velocity. Harnessing a power source capable of propelling us to such speeds currently lies well beyond our technological capability.

9.5. The Existence and Stability of Wormholes

Within the framework of general relativity, traversing through wormholes to distant regions of spacetime would be the simplest form of time travel, theoretically. However, wormholes are only hypothetical constructs, and their existence remains unproven. Moreover, even if one does exist, keeping it stable long enough for something or someone to pass through presents a significant challenge according to current scientific understanding.

Chapter 10. Paradoxes and Causality

After exploring the specific paradoxes and physical hurdles, a significant concern remains: the violation of causality. Time travel, particularly into the past, would introduce scenarios where the effect happens before the cause. This changes our understanding of cause-and-effect relationships, and repercussions would be significant, potentially including the unraveling of the fabric of reality.

In conclusion, time travel isn't merely a technological puzzle. It's a challenge that questions the fundamentals of our reality. While advances in theoretical physics and technology may one day provide answers, we currently stand in the realm of speculation. Yet the appeal of unraveling the mysteries of time remains irresistible. As we stand on the precipice of knowledge and discovery, time travel continues to provoke and inspire, challenging our perception of the universe in which we exist.

Chapter 11. Time Travel in Popular Culture: Science vs Fiction

Time travel has been a staple of popular culture for centuries, acting as the centerpiece for countless narratives within film, literature, and television. Yet, it stands at a crossroads where scientific theory meets imaginative speculation. To trace this intersection, one must trace the historical context, the roles time travel plays within storytelling, and the discrepancies and synchronicities between science and fiction.

11.1. Time Travel's Cinematic Journey

The realm of film has been an influential platform for exploring time travel. Georges Méliès' pioneering film "Le Voyage dans la Lune," (1902) is one of the earliest examples of cinematic time manipulation. However, it was H.G. Wells' "The Time Machine," published in 1895, and its subsequent film adaptations that pushed time travel to center stage, introducing audiences to the potential and pitfalls of moving through time.

As technology and scientific understanding progressed, so too did the portrayal of time travel in film. "Planet of the Apes" (1968) put a spin on time dilation, a concept theorizing time's relativity to gravitational pull and speed. In 1985, "Back to the Future" wove time travel into a coming-of-age narrative, highlighting potential paradoxes. It was considered groundbreaking for its depiction of altering and reshaping history through time travel.

Over the years, numerous movies have taken their own approaches to time travel, "The Terminator" (1984) depicted a loop in time where future and past are intrinsically linked, while "Interstellar" (2014) presented a scientifically-grounded interpretation of time dilation through a wormhole.

11.2. Page-turning Time Travel: From Wells to Murakami

Literature has long involved time travel, offering a playground for exploration unhindered by the necessities of visual representation. H.G Wells's novel drew attention to social critique and human nature through the guise of time travel, while Mark Twain's "A Connecticut Yankee in King Arthur's Court" (1889) leveraged time travel for comedic and satirical effect.

In contemporary literature, time travel is often used to explore existential themes. Haruki Murakami's "1Q84" (2009) features time as a mutable, permeable element where parallel realities co-exist and interpenetrate, presenting a sophisticated, mind-bending view. More recently, "The Psychology of Time Travel" (2018) by Kate Mascarenhas delves into the psychological outcomes of navigating through time, marrying science fiction with a painstaking character study.

11.3. Time Travel in Television: An Ongoing Series

Television has also been a robust medium for time travel narratives. Series like "Doctor Who" (1963-present) have tested the boundaries of time and space with countless adventures across centuries and galaxies. "Star Trek" (1966-1969) sparked audiences' fascinations with complex theories of space-time from various angles across its many timelines and spin-offs.

Recent series, such as "Dark" (2017-2020) and "The Umbrella

Academy" (2019-present), use time travel to dissect a convoluted web of cause and effect, demonstrating the genre's evolution into more complex portrayals of time manipulation.

11.4. Science in the Reel: Subversion or Emulation?

Against this backdrop of public fascination, where does science stand on time travel? Relativity theory, more specifically its special and general forms, laid a scientific basis for concepts of time travel. Albert Einstein's introduction of spacetime - the four-dimensional fabric of the Universe - was a groundbreaking scientific proclamation of time's malleability.

Scientists like Kip Thorne furthered Einstein's ideas by delving into the theory of wormholes, bridges through spacetime allowing for shortcuts through time and space. Stephen Hawking, however, cautioned regarding time paradoxes, like the infamous grandfather paradox that could occur with backwards time travel.

The common thread across these scientific theories is they are bound by laws of physics, and current engineering or technological constraints limit any practical application. However, these scientific ideas do often permeate popular culture, influencing the reality portrayed within cinematic, literary, and televised time travel.

Yet, discrepancies arise. For instance, depictions of time travel often serve plot over scientific accuracy, leading to inconsistent logic or rule-breaking within narratives. Events like the butterfly effect (change in past leading to significant change in future) or time loop paradoxes are imaginative manipulations, often divesting from scientific consensus.

11.5. Bridging Science and Fiction

Despite these differences, science and fiction interact dynamically, feeding off each other. While science provides a framework for representations of time travel, fiction fosters scenarios that stretch scientific understanding to its limits, and sometimes beyond.

In fact, time travel narratives may inspire scientific exploration. Fictional depictions of time travel, with their paradoxes and time warps, have led physicists to devise theories that reconcile these discrepancies. Scientists like Igor Novikov proposed the self-consistency principle, positing that any actions time travelers performed in the past would have already been part of history, thus avoiding any paradoxes.

11.6. Conclusion

In conclusion, while time travel in popular culture and the actual science of chronodynamics are two different entities, they converge in unexpected and stimulating ways. Films, novels, and television offer grand imaginations of manipulating time, bending it to fit narrative frameworks, often challenging or playing within scientific bounds.

As audiences, we remain fascinated by this interplay, gleaning understanding and wonder from both narrative constructs and scientific discourse. Time travel, as a concept, serves as a catalyst for this dialogue between science and fiction, bridging gaps and pushing limits in pursuit of understanding the fundamental fabric of our universe: time. Whether in the realm of fact or fiction, our journey through time, it seems, is only just beginning.

Chapter 12. The Ethics and Morality of Time Travel

Before we delve into how the principles of morality and ethics apply to time travel, it's essential to provide a brief overview of these concepts as they exist in our current understanding. Ethics, in essence, is the philosophical study that encompasses what is good, what is bad, right, wrong, and the rules and duties that should guide moral agents' behavior. Morality, on the other hand, is implicit rules and norms that define acceptable behavior within a society at a given time.

12.1. The Ethical Implications of Temporal Manipulation

Many ethical dilemmas are posed by the prospect of traveling through time. Imagine travelling back in time to alter a historical event. This action could potentially change the whole trajectory of human history, creating a ripple effect through time that might alter countless lives. We can consider this under the lens of consequentialism, a branch of ethics that judges morality based on actions' outcomes. If your action results in a more favorable outcome for the majority, one could argue it was justifiable. However, how can we accurately determine this when dealing with such a vast scale of impact?

Time travel also raises the concept of the non-identity problem. This ethical issue arises when one's actions in the past significantly alter individuals' identities in the present. For instance, a slight change in the past may lead to different people being born in the future, arguably making them different individuals altogether. The question then arises - is it ethical to change the identity of a person without their permission, even if they are yet to exist?

12.2. The Perils of Paradox

Central to the ethical considerations of time travel is the aspect of paradoxes, scenarios that defy logic or reason. The most well-known of these is the grandfather paradox. If a time traveler were to go back and inadvertently cause their grandfather's premature death, the traveler would not be born in the future, thereby negating their existence and their time-traveling intervention. This paradox exposes a key moral problem: whether or not time travelers have the right to alter events in the past that directly contradict and threaten their existence in the future.

The 'bootstrap' paradox presents another moral quagmire. In this paradox, an object or piece of information sent back in time becomes trapped within an infinite cause-effect loop. For example, a time traveler who gives Shakespeare an own-written copy of 'Hamlet', which the Bard then proceeds to 'write,' creates a loop where the play has no original author. Such a situation raises questions about originality, authorship, and how we value contributions to knowledge and culture.

12.3. Free Will, Determinism and Time Travel

The debate between free will and determinism also has profound implications for time travel. In a deterministic universe, every event, including your actions, are predetermined by previous events. Time travel in this context could create a fixed timeline where all events, including the time traveler's actions, are predestined - raising unsettling questions about the absence of free will and personal agency. On the other hand, the notion of multiple universes supports the idea of free will in time travel, allowing individuals to change the past without affecting their original timeline.

12.4. Moral Responsibility and Accountability in Time Travel

There's also the question of moral responsibility and accountability when it comes to time travel. If one travels back in time and makes changes, to what extent are they responsible for the consequences of their actions? If they change a historical event, is it justified to hold them accountable for the resulting changes in the timeline, especially when these changes could span generations and impact countless lives arbitrarily?

Similarly, time travel presents a predicament in terms of legal responsibility. Existing laws are confined to our current understanding of time and space. How then, would our legal systems hold someone accountable for actions committed in a different timeline, or a different period of history altogether?

This bring us to the end of our lengthy examination of the ethics and morality of time travel. Although we are currently not technologically equipped to navigate the complexities of the fourth dimension, the conceptual journey compels us to reevaluate our understanding of ethics and morality. As we ponder on these dilemmas and contradictions, we uncover further layers of our current ethical frameworks yet to be explored, demonstrating the profoundly introspective and mind-expanding potential of time travel. We find that time travel isn't just a reflection of our scientific aspirations but is also a mirror held up against our philosophical selves, offering a distinct prism through which to view, understand and interpret moral and ethical dilemmas. As our knowledge expands and we dare to push the boundaries of the known universe, we need to equip ourselves not just with scientific understanding, but with philosophical wisdom.

Chapter 13. The Future of Time Travel: Possibilities and Predictions

Space and time have intertwined us since the beginning of our consciousness. Time travel, the concept of moving between different points in time, has been a staple of science fiction for decades. Despite its fantastical premise, it has found a legitimate place within the scientific community, inspiring real-world scientific theories and research. The question now concerns not if time travel could be possible but rather when and how it can be achieved. As we stand at the precipice of this new frontier, we explore below the many possibilities and predictions surrounding the future of time travel.

13.1. Defining Time and Its Implications on Travel

Albert Einstein forever revolutionized our understanding of time in the early 20th century with his Special Theory of Relativity. He proposed that time and space aren't separate, but woven together in a four-dimensional fabric known as space-time.

In this configuration, time can be influenced by gravity, allowing it to speed up or slow down relative to another point. This is a phenomenon termed time dilation - a pillar of Einstein's General Theory of Relativity - and it is the primary concept that provides the theoretical basis for time travel.

However, these concepts open up a vast labyrinth of theoretical implications which, while not entirely undermining the potential for time travel, present thorny challenges that future research will have to tackle. For instance, the notion of a "time paradox" poses grave questions for the future of time travel. If one were to travel back in time and change past events, it could inarguably alter the present, creating a paradox. This creates the need for future research to investigate ways in which time travel could function while simultaneously avoiding such paradoxes.

13.2. Theoretical Advances Pave the Way

While paradoxes present a daunting roadblock, equally intriguing is the possibility of harnessing exotic matter or energy to resolve them. For instance, the hypothetical schematic of a wormhole could provide the necessary bridge through space-time without the threat of crushing or destabilizing matter within it. Utilizing these "shortcuts" through space-time, spawned from the theory of general relativity, could mean we are closer to making time travel a reality than ever before.

The existence of these wormholes is currently purely theoretical, but the pursuit to identify or even create these passages in space-time could become a key focus of future research. Similarly, advances in quantum mechanics could potentially allow for the existence of 'closed time-like curves' (CTCs), where an object follows a world line that eventually returns to its starting point in space-time, theoretically allowing for travel to the past.

13.3. The Role of Quantum Computing and Artificial Intelligence

As we weave through the fabric of space and time, it's crucial to understand the role technology, namely Quantum Computing and Artificial Intelligence (AI), could play in shaping time travel's future.

Quantum computing, with its computational prowess exceeding classical computing, opens up new pathways for simulating and understanding complex relativistic phenomena.

Furthermore, AI's rapid development could prove pivotal, particularly its ability to assist in calculating and managing the extraordinarily complex mathematical models which underpin time travel theories. Sophisticated algorithms could speed up our progression towards viable time travel by working to solve these enormous computational challenges.

13.4. Exploring Ethical and Societal Implications

Beyond the scientific and theoretic, the concept of time travel presents various ethical and societal implications which need comprehensive exploration before becoming a reality. These include the profound questions concerning altering historical events, the private ownership of time-travel technology, and the potential for misuse.

Protecting the timeline, avoiding negative historical revisionism, and preventing exploitation will be tasks as significant as the scientific challenges themselves. Comprehensive legislation and international cooperative agreements will have to be established that cover the use and regulation of time travel, similar in scope and seriousness to current agreements covering nuclear weapon use and space exploration.

13.5. Time Travel or Just Time Perception?

Finally, it's worth considering whether the idea of 'time travel' as it's typically understood is what we should be focusing on at all. An alternative approach could be shifting our focus to understanding and altering our perception of time. Some researchers suggest that instead of physically moving through time, manipulating the way our brains perceive and process time might be an easier (or simply more likely) approach.

The future of time travel is fraught with unknowns, both invigorating and intimidating. But it's clear that moving forward, the amalgamation of theoretical physics, advanced technology, and a comprehensive understanding of time's multidimensional qualities will push the boundaries of what we currently deem possible. Time travel has the potential to dramatically makeover our understanding of the universe, making it one of the most exciting frontiers of modern science. A profound era of discovery may await humanity if we can navigate the obstacles and unlock the temporal dimensions` secrets.

In conclusion, while far from a place where tickets could be reserved for a 'time-tour,' we're closer now more than ever to understanding the realities of time travel. Like Pandora's Box, time travel presents innumerable challenges and ethical considerations. And just as Pandora found hope at the bottom of her box, so might the scientific community find potential in the uncharted territory of time travel. The future – and indeed the past – are now emerging onto the horizon of scientific possibility. The allure of travelling through time will continue to captivate our collective imagination, spurring further research and presenting endless scientific possibilities.